THE REVEREND MR. PUNCH

THE REVEREND MR. PUNCH

Pictorial Record of a Sixty Years' Ministry

COMPILED BY

MICHAEL EDWARDES

LONDON
A. R. MOWBRAY & Co. LIMITED

First published in 1956

PRINTED IN GREAT BRITAIN BY
A. R. MOWBRAY & CO. LIMITED IN THE CITY OF OXFORD
6452

FOREWORD

THE 'Reverend' Mr. Punch! Perhaps a little ironic, for the cartoons I have selected may appear to lack reverence. Some are even a trifle cutting. But here we have again the proof that *Punch* is very much the mirror of English humour, and, because of it, a mirror of English life. Distorted a little, of course, for satire is only the normal slightly out of focus—the improbable situation we sometimes *do* find ourselves involved in, the coming-together of impossibles accidentally noticed in the street just after we have decided how silly it would be. Here they are as regards parish and clergy, beginning with the well-known joke about the 'Curate's Egg' and going on to the *Punch* of to-day.

I have tried to make these cartoons reflect the attitudes of *Punch*—and its readers—to the clergy over the past sixty years or so. The choice is an arbitrary one, but I believe this collection does represent a piece of social history, a backstair of our times. Throughout, the 'parson' is satirized, but there is an almost steady progress from 'laughing at' to 'laughing with.' Times change and now we smile for different reasons. The knife is rusty but it still cuts.

Only the English, it is said, could produce *Punch*. Only the English (I should write 'British') can afford to laugh at the things they cherish most. In all these cartoons, however sharp the humour, the joke emerges from a well-tried love, and what is love, after all, but one of the most reverend of all things?

I ought to add that there is necessarily an obvious disproportion in the space given to different decades. It arises from the fact that fashions change, and that at times *Punch* has given less attention to the cloth and the parish than at others.

MICHAEL EDWARDES

INDEX OF ARTISTS

ACKNOWLEDGEMENT

Cordial thanks are due to the Proprietors of PUNCH, with whose kind permission and co-operation this collection of PUNCH drawings is published.

Nov. 9, 1895

G. du Maurier

TRUE HUMILITY

Right Reverend Host. 'I'm afraid you've got a bad Egg, Mr. Jones!'

The Curate. 'Oh no, my Lord, I assure you! Parts of it are excellent!'

THE BISHOP'S SERMON

The Bishop's Wife (to the Vicaress who is getting drowsy). 'May I lend you my Smelling Salts?'

The Vicaress. 'Oh no, thanks! I would much rather go to sleep!'

Sept. 5, 1896   G. du Maurier

Nov. 7, 1896   L. Raven-Hill

Rector. 'Now, what *you* want, my good Man, is Oxygen, plenty of Oxygen.'

Giles (brightening up). 'Law now, is it, Sir? An' thankye kindly. I can't say as I ever tasted *that* sort o' gin, but I'll ask for it over to the "Three Tuns." '

Aug. 8, 1896   G. du Maurier

TANTÆ NE ANIMIS CŒ LESTIBUS IRÆ?

'What a shocking bad appointment to the Deanery of Barchester!'

'Oh—I don't know. The usual qualifications: own brother to a Peer, and a failure wherever he had been before!'

Jan. 16, 1897 *H. G. Jalland*

MUSIC HATH CHARMS

Rector's Daughter. 'You haven't joined the Choral Class, Mr. Harrington. We have such fun, you know.'

Bachelor Squire. 'Choral Class! Why I haven't an atom of Voice!'

Rector's Daughter. 'Oh, that doesn't matter in the least. We none of us have! Do come!'

May 15, 1897   *Bernard Partridge*

AFTER MANY YEARS!

Country Parson (*to distinguished Peer, who has been making* THE *Speech of the evening*). 'How d'ye do, my Lord? I see you don't quite remember me.'

Distinguished Peer. 'Well—er—not altogether.'

C.P. 'We were Members of the same Club at Oxford.'

D.P. (*with awakening interest*). 'Oh—ah! Let me see—which Club was that?'

C.P. 'The—er—*Toilet Club*, you know!'

13

SQUARING ACCOUNTS

Cabbie (*on receipt of his legal fare*). 'All right, my Lud! I can jis stop a trifle out of my Sunday Orfferins!'

'WHAT'S IN A NAME?'

(A Sketch at a Regatta. A warning to 'the Cloth' when up the River.)

THE FIRST LESSON

Little Boy (*in Church for the first time*). 'Oh, Gran'ma, what is he going to do to Polly?'

June 13, 1900   *S. C. Vosper*

Apr. 30, 1898   *Arthur Hopkins*

MISUNDERSTOOD!

Mrs. Van de Leur. 'By the way, Mr. Fairfax, if any of my Son's old Boots would be of use to you. . . .'

Mr. Fairfax (*interrupting*). 'Really, Madam! The Clergy *are* underpaid, but we can. . . .'

> [Rises to take his leave. But Mrs. Van de Leur was only thinking of the Ragged School.]

A 'CALCULATING BOY!'

Tommy (in audible whisper). 'Mummy, they've added it up right for the first time!'

June 17, 1903   *F. G. Lewin*

Dec. 26, 1900   *L. Raven-Hill*

Agricultural Parishioner (wishing to ingratiate himself with the new Curate, who had given a Lecture on the previous evening). 'Thank ye, Sir, for your reading to us last night.'

New Curate. 'Glad you liked it, John. I was a little afraid lest the lecture might have been just a *little* too scientific.'

Agricultural Parishioner. 'No, bless you, Sir, not a bit of it. Why, we in these parts be just like young ducks. *We do gobble up anything!*'

Feb. 20, 1901

Lewis Baumer

Visitor to Country Town (*who has been shown over the Church*). 'And how long has your present Vicar been here?'

Sexton. 'Mr. Mole, Sir, has been the *Incumbrance* here, Sir, for nigh on forty year, Sir!'

Apr. 22, 1903

L. Raven-Hill

Curate. You're looking very well to-day, Mrs. Giles.'

Chronic Grumbler. 'Ah, but you ain't a-seen my inside, Sir!'

Missionary (who is really a 'good plucked 'un,' though he doesn't look it). 'Our Station was so remote that for a whole year my wife never saw a White Face but my own!'

Sympathetic Young Woman. 'Oh, poor thing!'

May 20, 1903

Phil May

Aug. 12, 1903   *Lewis Baumer*

Vicar of Country Parish (interviewing new verger). 'Now, Mr. Jones, with regard to the Collections. When there is a Sermon, I shall want you to make the Collection immediately after; and when . . .'

Mr. Jones (anxious to appear intelligent). 'Yessir, I quite understand you, Sir; and when there is not a Sermon, Sir, the Collection takes place *immediately before*!'

Scene—*Country Vicarage*

Burglar (*who has been secured by athletic Vicar after long and severe struggle*). 'I think you're treatin' me very crool—and a *Clergyman* too!'

Sept. 23, 1903   *L. L. B.*

June 22, 1904   G. D. Armour

TEACHING THE TEACHER

New Curate. 'Now Boy, if, in defiance of that notice, *I* were to bathe here, what do you suppose would happen?'

Boy. 'You'd come out a great lot dirtier than you went in!'

Aug. 23, 1905

A QUESTION OF VESTED INTEREST

Vicar. 'Well, Gentlemen, what can I do for you?'

Spokesman. 'Please, Sir, we be a deputation from Farmers down Froglands Parish, to ask you to pray for fine weather for t'arvest.'

Vicar. 'Why don't you ask your own Vicar?'

Spokesman. 'Well, Sir, we reckon 'e be'unt much good for this 'ere. 'E do be that fond of Fishin'.'

Jan. 10, 1906

Gunning King

Parson. 'Good morning, Mrs. Stubbins. Is your husband at home?'

Mrs. Stubbins. ' 'E's 'ome, Sir; but 'e's a-bed.'

Parson. 'How is it he didn't come to Church on Sunday? You know we must have our hearts in the right place.'

Mrs. Stubbins. 'Lor, Sir, 'is 'eart's all right. It's 'is Trowziz!'

Feb. 7, 1906

L. Raven-Hill

THINGS ONE WOULD RATHER HAVE EXPRESSED DIFFERENTLY

Our Curate (who is going to describe to us his little holiday in Lovely Lucerne). 'My dear friends—I will not call you "Ladies and Gentlemen," since I know you too well——'

23

Shepperton

Vicar. 'I am so glad your dear daughter is better. I was greatly pleased to see her in church this morning, and shortened the service on purpose for her.'

Mother of dear daughter. 'Thank you, Vicar. I shall hope to bring her every Sunday now!'

July 24, 1907   *Gunning King*

AT OUR CHURCH BAZAAR

Vicar (effusively to conductor at close of a brilliant programme). The music sounded very delightful in the distance, and I can assure you it did not in any way interfere with the sales!'

DETECTED

Clerical Tourist (visiting Cathedral). 'Always open, eh? And do you find that people come here on weekdays for rest and meditation?'

Verger. 'Ay, that they do, odd times, Why, I catched some of 'em at it only last Toosday!'

Feb. 14, 1906   *Townsend*

DISTRESSING OCCURRENCE
IN OUR PARISH

Bobbie (who has been taken to Harvest Festival, but is considered too young to stay for the sermon—fortissimo). 'Boo-hoo—I-want-to-stop-to-dessert!'

Oct. 23, 1907   Lewis Baumer

'Will you excuse me, Mother, if I don't go in with you? You see, Father said I was to live within my means, and I don't feel as if I could afford the collection!'

Dec. 4, 1907   *Gunning King*

26

Feb. 27, 1907   *Gunning King*

OUR RECTOR RECEIVES A PRESENTATION

'My friends, your kindness has followed me throughout my sojourn in your midst, but never till now has it overtaken me!'

Clergyman (by way of consoling despondent parishioner). 'Just consider how you have been guided and provided for all these seventy years.'

Parishioner. 'Sixty-nine, *if* you please!'

Oct. 16, 1907   *A. S. Boyd*

Jan. 22, 1908

Lawson Wood

Vicar. 'John, do you—er—ever use strong language?'

John (*guardedly*). 'Well, Sir, I—I may be a little bit keerless like in my speech at times.'

Vicar. 'Ah, I'm sorry, John. But we will converse about that some other time. Just now I want you to go to the plumber's and settle this bill of four pounds ten for thawing out a water-pipe. And you might just talk to the man in a careless sort of way, as if it were your own bill!'

Mar. 4, 1908

Fred Pegram

Vicar. 'Well, Mary, I was very surprised to see John walk out in the middle of the sermon yesterday!'

Mary. 'Ah, Sir, I do 'ope you'll excuse my poor 'usband. 'E's a terrible one for walkin' in 'is sleep.'

July 8, 1908

Gunning King

Jim (regarding damage done to church by fire). 'Good job it wasn't a factory, Bill.'

Bill. 'You're right, mate. Only one man put out of work, and *he* draws his money!'

Old Gentleman. 'Very charming old sedilia you have here.'

Caretaker. 'Yes, Sir, you ain't by no means the fust as 'as admired 'em. That's where the clergymen used to sit, in the order of their senility.'

Feb. 26, 1908   *Gunning King*

Apr. 8, 1908   *Charles Crombie*

'Now, my good man, you mustn't bring your wheelbarrow through here. You must go round the other way. Aren't you aware that this is consecrated ground?'

'Well, Zur, I didn't knaw but what the barry warn't consecrated too. I borry'd it o' the sexton.'

31

Aug. 19, 1908   *Gunning King*

Parson (discovering odd-job man working at the chapel). 'Why, Giles, I was not aware that you cut the grass for the dissenters too?'

Giles. 'Well, your reverence, I does sometimes; but *I don't use the same scythe!*'

Mar. 3, 1909   *Gunning King*

Curate (who struggles to exist on £120 *a year with wife and six children).* 'We are giving up meat as a little experiment, Mrs. Dasher.'

Wealthy Parishioner. 'Oh, yes! One can *so well* live on fish, poultry, game, and plenty of nourishing wines, can't one?'

Mar. 30, 1910   C. E. Brock

The Vicar. 'Well, Giles, did you find my lecture dry last night?'

Giles. 'Well, Sir, I wouldn't go so fur as to say that, but when you stops in the middle to 'ev a swig, though it was only water, I ses to my missus, " 'Ear, 'ear." '

July 20, 1910   *A. Wallis Mills*

New Vicar's Wife (who has just come from her first Mothers' Meeting). 'And, my dear, you can't think *how* nice some of the women are. *Far* too respectable to be mothers, I'm sure!'

C   33

July 17, 1912   Frank Reynolds

Our Captain. 'Decent of him to carry the bags.'
Our Vice. 'Yes; I suppose he'll expect to play now.'

May 10, 1911   F. H. T.

OUR AMENDE

(*Mr. Punch* has received several complaints about the slovenliness in dress of the clergymen depicted in his pages. He cannot any longer lie under this reproach and has specially summoned his fashion artist from Mayfair to put in the clerical figure above.)

The Countess Blenkinsop (supported by the Earl Blenkinsop, Captain Lord Ranelagh, Lady Ermyntrude D'Arcy-Osborne, and the Hon. Algernon D'Arcy-Osborne, to their guest, the Rev. Septimus Brocade). 'We are quite simple people, Mr. Brocade, and we do hope you won't feel that we expect you to change your clothes for tea.'

Apr. 5, 1911   *Ernest H. Shepard*

'How do you like the Vicar?'

'Not at all; he's so fat—and in Lent, too!'

Sept. 27, 1911

A. Wallis Mills

The Rector. 'Now, Molly, would you rather be beautiful or good?'

Molly. 'I'd rather be beautiful and repent.'

July 24, 1912

G. L. Stampa

The Vicar's Son (who was greatly interested in the Bishop's visit yesterday, and has been solemnly inspecting lady's ankles). 'Oh, I s'pose you're the wife of the bishop?'

Oct. 9, 1912   *G. J.*

A COMPROMISE

Country Vicar (*returning from service*). 'Is Parliament sitting now, my dear?'
Wife. 'I don't know.'
Vicar. 'Nor I; that's why I said the prayer for Parliament in such a low voice.'

Apr. 9, 1913   *George Belcher*

'I am glad to see you come so regularly to our evening services, Mrs. Brown.'
'Yus. Yer see, me 'usband 'ates me goin' hout of a hevening, so I does it to spite 'im.'

Mar. 29, 1916 *George Belcher*

The Vicar. 'These Salonikans, Mrs. Stubbs, are of course the Thessalonians to whom St. Paul wrote his celebrated letters.'

Mrs. Stubbs. 'Well, I 'ope 'e'd better luck with 'is than *I* 'ave. *I* sent my boy out there three letters and two parcels, and I ain't got no answer yet.'

Apr. 17, 1918 *A. Wallis Mills*

Hostess. 'I think the dear Vicar has the face of a martyr. Don't you?'

Visitor. 'Indeed he has. And wouldn't he look just *sweet* burning at the stake?'

40

OUR HARVEST FESTIVAL

Humorist (*in stage whisper*). 'Vicar looks rather well in his allotment.'

Oct. 23, 1918   *G. L. Stampa*

THE REV SILVANUS JONES
WILL PREACH
NEXT SUNDAY MORNING
ON
WHAT'S WRONG
WITH
THE CHURCH?

THE QUESTION OF THE HOUR

Nov. 14, 1917   *F. H. T.*

J.H.DOWD.20

Mar. 16, 1921   *J. H. Dowd*

Examining Bishop (*to eligible bachelor curate during reading test*). 'I can't hear you.'

Curate. 'I'm sorry, my lord; but if I may say so, I understood I could be heard quite well; so my audience at the mission tells me.'

Bishop. 'Does she?'

July 13, 1921   *Bert Thomas*

Wife. 'Did you notice the chinchilla coat on the woman sitting in front of us this morning?'

Husband. 'Er—no. Afraid I was dozing most of the time.'

Wife. 'Um. A lot of good the service did *you*.'

July 13, 1921   *Bernard Partridge*

Villager. 'There goes our curate. Nice quiet gentleman 'e was till 'e took up with a motor-bike; but now 'e don't 'alf rush 'is sermons.'

Jan. 4, 1922   *L. Raven-Hill*

Hostess. 'And what good resolutions have *you* made for the New Year?'

Aug. 30, 1922   *Treyer Evans*

A BROADCASTING PERIL
Time—*Sunday Morning*

Vicar. 'This is terrible! Five minutes before the service and not a soul here!'

Verger. 'No, Sir; but I understand there are some thousands waiting in their own homes to "listen in." '

'Mummy, what *was* the Vicar asking when he read out those names?'

'Oh, you mean the Banns of Marriage!'

'Well, why was he so cross about it? He said, "This is the *second* time I've asked you." '

Nov. 14, 1923   *George Belcher*

Newly-appointed Rector. 'I say, our policeman's a sportsman. He caught me without a light last night. I gave him half a crown and he let me off.'

Squire and Local J.P. 'My dear fellow, you shouldn't do that—a shilling's ample.'

Mar. 14, 1923   *A. T. Smith*

46

July 19, 1922   *A. Wallis Mills*

Vicar (returning thanks to village benefactress for entertainment). 'I am sure you will all join with me in thanking her ladyship for throwing open her park to us this afternoon, and also join me in the earnest hope that she will be spared for many years to throw open the park, and that the park will be spared for many years to be—ah—thrown open.'

Jan. 23, 1924   *George Belcher*

Church Cleaner. 'Popular preacher, indeed! I've no patience with 'im. We never 'ad all this mud in the church afore 'e come.'

Jan. 27, 1926   *George Belcher*

Wife of Church Dignitary (meeting friend at the Zoo). 'Oh, how do you do? I'm looking for the Prebendary. You haven't seen him, have you?'

Friend. 'No, I haven't.'

Helpful Stranger. 'Pardon me, Madam; I expect they'll be next to the ostriches— over there.'

OUR VICAR'S WIFE BUYS A NEW HAT.

Sept. 21, 1927

Arthur Watts

Feb. 26, 1930

George Belcher

Daughter of Clergyman who has just become a Doctor of Divinity. 'Is that lady-doctor one of those that make people better, or is she like Daddy?'

July 15, 1931   *Treyer Evans*

First Boy. 'What's them strings on 'is 'at?'
Second Boy. 'Wireless, o' course.'

July 15, 1931   *Frank R. Grey*

Absent-minded Vicar (receiving large vegetable-marrow for decoration of the font at Harvest Festival). 'Is it a little boy or girl?'

51

Nov. 6, 1929

D. L. Ghilchip

Fiancée. 'After we're married, dear, you won't mind if I don't come to your church much, will you?'

Curate. 'But why ever not, precious?'

Fiancée. 'Well, you see, I don't really approve of married clergymen.'

The Vicar. 'You suspect hashish? But, good heavens, man, look at my collar!'

Zealous Customs. 'Yess, yess— plentytime I search you under the collar in a minute.'

Sept. 21, 1932   *Chas. Grave*

'The organist says would you mind not singing so loud, Sir, as we're broadcasting this service, and you're messing up the balance of the choir?'

July 17, 1935   *Chas. Grave*

Feb. 7, 1934   *L. Raven-Hill*

'And what do you think of the European situation, Mrs. Brown?'

'Oh, I'm quite content to leave such things in the hands of the Vicar.'

'You must excuse my whispering, but I've had a cold and lost my voice.'

'That's a bad job, Sir, for a man as earns 'is living by 'ollering.'

Feb. 17, 1937   *George Belcher*

Feb. 7, 1934　　　　　　　　　　　　　　　　　　　　　　　　*George Belcher*

'It's wonderful what the hand of man can do to a piece of earth, with the aid of Divine Providence, Wilks.'

'You should 'ave seen this piece, Sir, when Divine Providence 'ad it all to itself.'

Mar. 16, 1938   *Frank Reynolds*

'John, dear, will you please help the poached eggs?'

'Gladly, my dear. What sort of assistance do they require?'

Sept. 21, 1938   *Sillince*

'. . . and Sir Francis has ordered a case of best Australian apples from Covent Garden for your Harvest Festival.'

Jan. 24, 1951

Acanthus

'Would you kindly settle an argument—is this, or is it not, the longest nave in Britain?'

Dec. 23, 1953   *William Scully*

'Not *the* Dr. Kinsey?'

Nov. 11, 1953   *Mervyn Wilson*

58

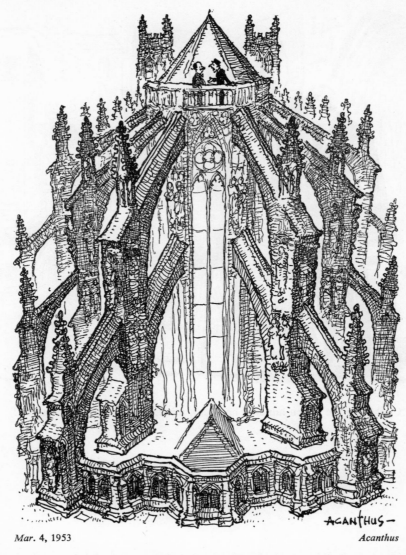

Mar. 4, 1953   *Acanthus*

'You'd never think this cathedral is supported almost entirely by voluntary contributions.'

Apr. 21, 1948   *Anton*

'Could you use fifteen hundred hassocks, mister—and no questions asked?'

July 2, 1947   Anton

'Same address, I presume, sir—St. Mark's Vicarage, near Newmarket?'

'He's one of the few in favour of it.'

July 15, 1953   David Langdon

61

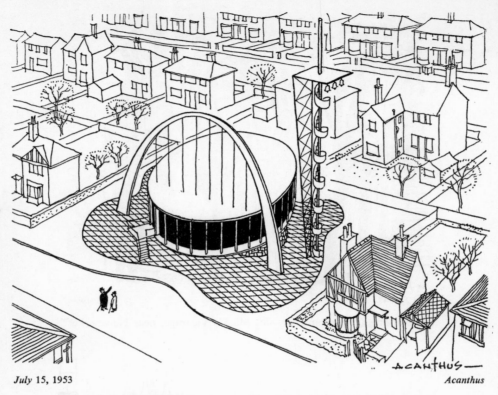

July 15, 1953

Acanthus

'They wanted to erect a factory, but fortunately Vicar got his own way.'

Mar. 10, 1954

David Langdon

'I'm no Billy Graham . . .'

Oct. 12, 1955   David Langdon

'Many conversions this week?'